FOUNDED BY WILLIAM MORRIS IN 1861

MORRIS & Co

Designs & Patterns

from the

Art Gallery of South Australia

Foreword

he Art Gallery of South Australia holds the largest Morris & Co. collection outside Britain. Most of the collecting of this material has taken place since 1989. Such an achievement seems almost impossible to imagine since William Morris has long been recognised as an iconic British designer. However, Adelaide's unique circumstances made it possible. From 1884 to 1929 the immensely wealthy Adelaide couple, Robert and Joanna Barr Smith, and their family were major international clients of Morris's London shop, furnishing seven of their vast South Australian houses almost exclusively from the firm. Members of the Rymill, Brookman and Dutton families were other progressive Adelaide clients of Morris & Co. which meant a superb wealth of material was shipped to South Australia. Large quantities of hand-knotted carpets, rugs, tapestries, embroideries, soft furnishings, furniture, wallpapers and fabrics were ordered, and although some have been lost through the ravages of time, much remains. Morris's unwavering hand-made quality products, coupled with careful ownership has enabled a richly diverse collection to be accumulated through the generosity of gifts and gallery acquisitions.

The twenty-nine designs selected for this resource book are drawn largely from this unique Adelaide provenance, with the exception of a few recent examples purchased directly from London. I wish to thank Robert Reason, the Curator of Decorative Arts, for his insightful observations on each work. A full account of the gallery's extensive Morris & Co. holdings is available in Christopher Menz's fully illustrated book *Morris & Co.*, published in 2002 by the Art Gallery of South Australia. I trust you will find the *Morris & Co. Designs & Patterns* inspiring and beneficial when commencing upon your own design project.

Ron Radford
Director, Art Gallery of South Australia, Adelaide

Introduction

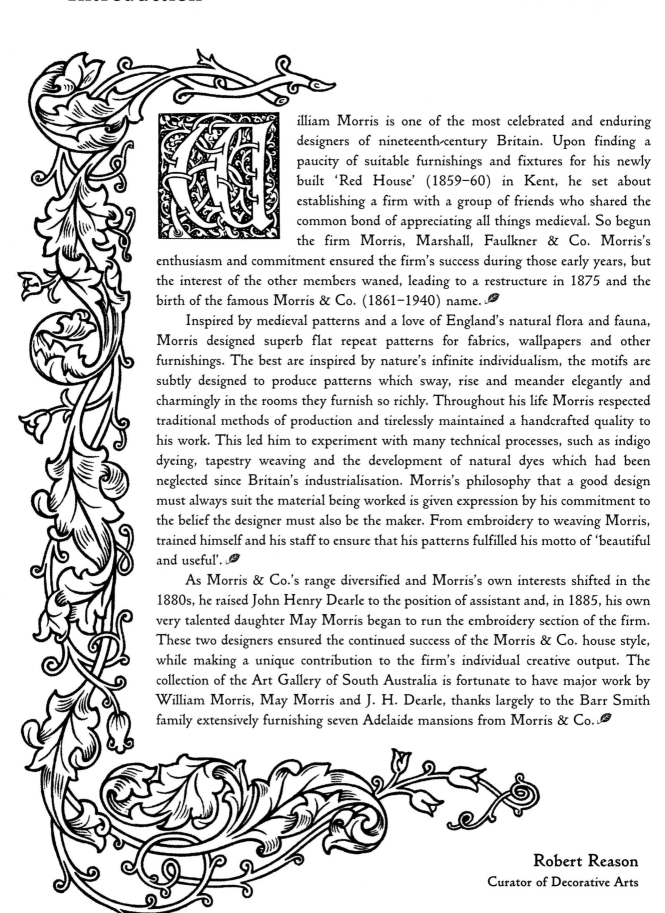

William Morris is one of the most celebrated and enduring designers of nineteenth-century Britain. Upon finding a paucity of suitable furnishings and fixtures for his newly built 'Red House' (1859–60) in Kent, he set about establishing a firm with a group of friends who shared the common bond of appreciating all things medieval. So begun the firm Morris, Marshall, Faulkner & Co. Morris's enthusiasm and commitment ensured the firm's success during those early years, but the interest of the other members waned, leading to a restructure in 1875 and the birth of the famous Morris & Co. (1861–1940) name.

Inspired by medieval patterns and a love of England's natural flora and fauna, Morris designed superb flat repeat patterns for fabrics, wallpapers and other furnishings. The best are inspired by nature's infinite individualism, the motifs are subtly designed to produce patterns which sway, rise and meander elegantly and charmingly in the rooms they furnish so richly. Throughout his life Morris respected traditional methods of production and tirelessly maintained a handcrafted quality to his work. This led him to experiment with many technical processes, such as indigo dyeing, tapestry weaving and the development of natural dyes which had been neglected since Britain's industrialisation. Morris's philosophy that a good design must always suit the material being worked is given expression by his commitment to the belief the designer must also be the maker. From embroidery to weaving Morris, trained himself and his staff to ensure that his patterns fulfilled his motto of 'beautiful and useful'.

As Morris & Co.'s range diversified and Morris's own interests shifted in the 1880s, he raised John Henry Dearle to the position of assistant and, in 1885, his own very talented daughter May Morris began to run the embroidery section of the firm. These two designers ensured the continued success of the Morris & Co. house style, while making a unique contribution to the firm's individual creative output. The collection of the Art Gallery of South Australia is fortunate to have major work by William Morris, May Morris and J. H. Dearle, thanks largely to the Barr Smith family extensively furnishing seven Adelaide mansions from Morris & Co.

Robert Reason
Curator of Decorative Arts

Designs & Patterns

The following designs from Morris & Co. are grouped by media and ordered chronologically by the date of their design.

Tulip fabric

Designed by Morris in 1875, this block-printed cotton was manufactured for Morris & Co. by Thomas Wardle of Leek who did all of Morris's printed textiles between 1875 and 1878. The *Tulip* design is based on simple rectangular segments, each containing a swaying tulip bloom and dense foliage. They form alternating rows of open and closed flowers in which the direction of the flower stem and foliage is inverted. The flat pattern and design structure has much in common with *Marigold* which was printed in the same year.

    Tulip was available in over ten colourways including grey, green, red and the blue reproduced here. Available in 91.5 cm widths, with a repeat pattern of 54.5 x 23.0 cm, it was ideal for curtains and upholstered furniture. The William Morris Gallery in Walthamstow, London, has in its collection the original design and its twelve printing blocks.

Crown imperial curtain

Designed by Morris in 1876, the *Crown imperial* pattern is strictly formal by comparison with his later free-flowing designs, such as *Evenlode*. A monochromatic jacquard woven fabric, the mohair damask created the necessary sheen for the pattern to stand out from the wool. The damask tendrils in *Crown imperial* successfully carry the repeating pattern of enclosed bunches of flowers and leaves. In biblical history the crown imperial flower was the one that refused to bow its head at the Crucifixion, and has wept ever since. It was available in a variety of colourways and was aptly suitable as curtain fabric.

Bird curtain

Bird was designed by William Morris in 1878 and is one of four woven textiles featuring pairs of birds. A year earlier, Morris had written to Thomas Wardle expressing his desire to incorporate birds into his upcoming designs and sought Wardle's help in establishing a textiles workshop. For this fabric Morris designed the birds in pairs, perching on the interlocking floral background and flying with front wings touching. The pattern was inspired by Italian woven silks from the sixteenth and seventeenth centuries, housed in the collection of the South Kensington Museum (now the Victoria & Albert Museum) where Morris was an adviser.

The fabric is thick woollen double cloth with the two warps and wefts interchanged across the pattern so that the cloth layers were held together. *Bird* was popular with many clients who used it for curtains, but Morris swathed his whole drawing room at Kelmscott House with the fabric. His daughter May, described it as 'intimate and friendly ... the most adaptable to the needs of everyday life.'

Peacock & dragon curtain

The Morris & Co. catalogue *Silk and Wool Tapestries, Brocades etc* (1912) comments: 'This fine design, which was a favourite with its author, requires a large room to set off its proportions. It is essentially Gothic in character, and carried out in low-toned schemes of colour ... it makes a perfect hanging for a medieval castle or a mansion.'

Designed by William Morris in 1878 and made of heavy woven wool, *Peacock & dragon* created a patterned floral background with pairs of inward facing birds in alternating rows across the width of the fabric. The massive repeat of the pattern – 109.0 x 90.0 cm – meant it was ideal for large curtains and as a complete wall covering. It came in a variety of colours, and although the inspiration for the design is from the Near and Far East, Morris considered it to be in the spirit of English medieval hangings.

Dove & rose curtain

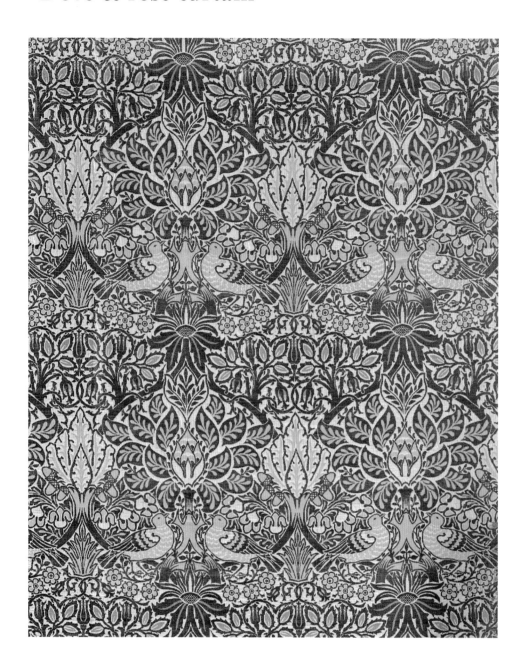

This is one of Morris's most luxurious hand-woven cloths, providing clients with an eye-catching pattern of silk and wool threads woven together and separately. The result is a fabric of shimmering silk highlights on a durable wool double cloth. Designed in 1879, it followed the successful Morris patterns *Bird* and *Peacock & dragon* from the prior year.

The specialist skills involved with its production required *Dove & rose* to be woven by Alexander Morton & Co. in Scotland. The cloth was available in a number of colours and a variety of pattern sizes. The structure of the fabric made it most suitable for curtains and hangings. ✒

Brer rabbit fabric

Brer rabbit or *Brother rabbit* as it is otherwise known, was designed by Morris and registered in 1882 as an indigo discharge and blocked printed cotton. Morris's rabbits' crouch amongst acanthus-style leaves, with alternating rows of singing birds in trees. Philip Webb, a friend of Morris's, is credited for designing the bird and rabbit in this textile. Webb had designed the birds in Morris's first wallpaper *Trellis* in 1862. May Morris in her 1936 book on her father, however, states that Morris was fully responsible for all aspects of *Brer rabbits* design.

    Brer rabbit is one of three patterns, the others being *Bird & anemone* and *Rose & thistle,* that Morris had designed ready to be printed when the Merton Abbey workshop came on-line in 1882. All three were produced in indigo discharge, with the design in white. *Brer rabbit* was available in a number of other colourways, including the striking red illustrated here.

Windrush fabric

Morris started designing *Windrush* in 1881 but it was not registered until October 1883. Block-printed onto the surface of cotton and linen, this example was originally from a curtain. Morris sent his designs to Thomas Wardle's block-cutters, Alfred Barrett and later, James Barrett, who used tracing paper to copy the designs and transfer them to pearwood blocks. Morris checked all tracings, since blocks had to be cut for each colour and carefully matched to ensure the correct registration of the design.

Windrush moves away from representational depictions of flowers and leaves to complex figure-of-eight patterns created by interwoven plant stems. Note that of the two flower heads, one contains an elaborate internal pattern which Morris described as 'the inhabited leaf'. Persian and Turkish carpets were his source for this decorative motif.

Evenlode curtain

Evenlode is one of the early indigo discharge-printed fabrics to come out of Morris's own Merton Abbey Workshop in 1883. William Morris drew the pattern at his Kelmscott House while suffering gout. In a letter written to May Morris in March 1883, he expressed having trouble finding a suitable name. In the end, he settled on 'Evenlode', making it the first Morris & Co. design to be named after a tributary of the river Thames. A further six designs were named after tributaries and have similarly meandering stems with leaves and flower heads.

Evenlode contains a variety of flowers in horizontal rows, although the pattern is vertical in emphasis due to repeat waving bands of flower stems. The pattern made it particularly suitable for tied-back curtains as the undulating curve worked well across the folds of the fabric. The inspiration for the effect came from seventeenth-century Italian brocaded velvets Morris saw at the South Kensington Museum in 1883. Thirty-three wood blocks were required to print the *Evenlode* design, which was used on upholstered furniture and as curtain fabric. 🖋

Medway curtain

The practical labour of drawing patterns was cherished by Morris, and moving to Merton Abbey (June 1881) gave him impetus to develop fresh designs. At the new workshop he began experimenting with 'dipping,' or what we know as the indigo-dyeing process. Between 1882 and 1885 seventeen designs were registered as using indigo discharge, with *Medway* being designed by Morris in 1885.

The *Medway* design was printed onto cotton through a series of set stages and was suitable for curtains. The first stage involved the cotton being submerged into the indigo dye vat and, following its removal, a bleaching agent was block-printed onto the flat cloth to create the patterned areas not intended to be blue. The dominant pattern of undulating lines of tendrils and flowers was then repeatedly block-printed for each colour. The overall effect was one that Morris favoured – a small subsidiary flower design against the indigo discharge, with a repeating bold diagonal structured stem-and-flower design.

Rose & lily curtain

Over a period of thirty-four years J. H. Dearle was responsible for thirty original designs at Morris & Co., his most imaginative period being 1888 to 1905. *Rose & lily* was designed by Dearle in 1893, while still under the direction of William Morris and was hand-loom jacquard-woven at the Merton Abbey workshop. The fabric is a blend of woven silk and wool and was available in four colourways – white, blue, red or dark green grounds.

Like Morris, Dearle used the textile collection at the South Kensington Museum as a design resource. His passion for historic textiles is clearly expressed in *Rose & lily*, which has as its source Italian seventeenth-century brocaded silks. Instead of Italian crowns, Dearle substitutes roses, whose thorny stems create an ogee pattern framing two types of lilies. The pattern is completed in coloured silks, giving the fabric a rich and sensual effect. 🍃

Compton curtain

This design was one of J. H. Dearle's finest, and dates from 1896, the year William Morris died. Dearle began work with Morris & Co. in 1878, at their Oxford Street shop in London. Morris, 'influenced by the evident intelligence and brightness of the boy' was soon to train him as the first apprentice tapestry weaver. By the late 1880s Dearle was supplying his own designs to Morris & Co.

    Compton's printing blocks were alternated between producing wallpapers and fabrics. The pattern name came from the interior decoration scheme Dearle supplied for Compton Hall in the West Midlands of England. *Compton* is a beautiful scrolling diagonal pattern with a variety of flowers, buds and leaves in hues of blue, pink and green. Printed on cotton, *Compton* was suitable for curtains and as slip-covers for soft furnishings.

Trellis wallpaper

Wallpaper was the second serial production item for Morris, Marshall, Faulkner & Co. after glass tableware. By the end of his life William Morris had overseen the printing of approximately seventy designs of which at least fifty were his own. All his wallpapers were printed by the traditional wood-block process and contracted out to Jeffrey & Co., a wallpaper specialist.

Trellis, along with *Daisy*, were Morris's first wallpapers to be registered in February 1864. The original design for *Trellis* was conceived by Morris in 1862, who arranged for his close friend the designer and architect, Philip Webb, to draw the birds for his trailing rose-clad trellis. The formal feature of the trellis was inspired by medieval motifs, but also directly from his own passionate interest in gardening at Red House during the early 1860s. Morris later had this pattern installed in his bedroom at Kelmscott House.

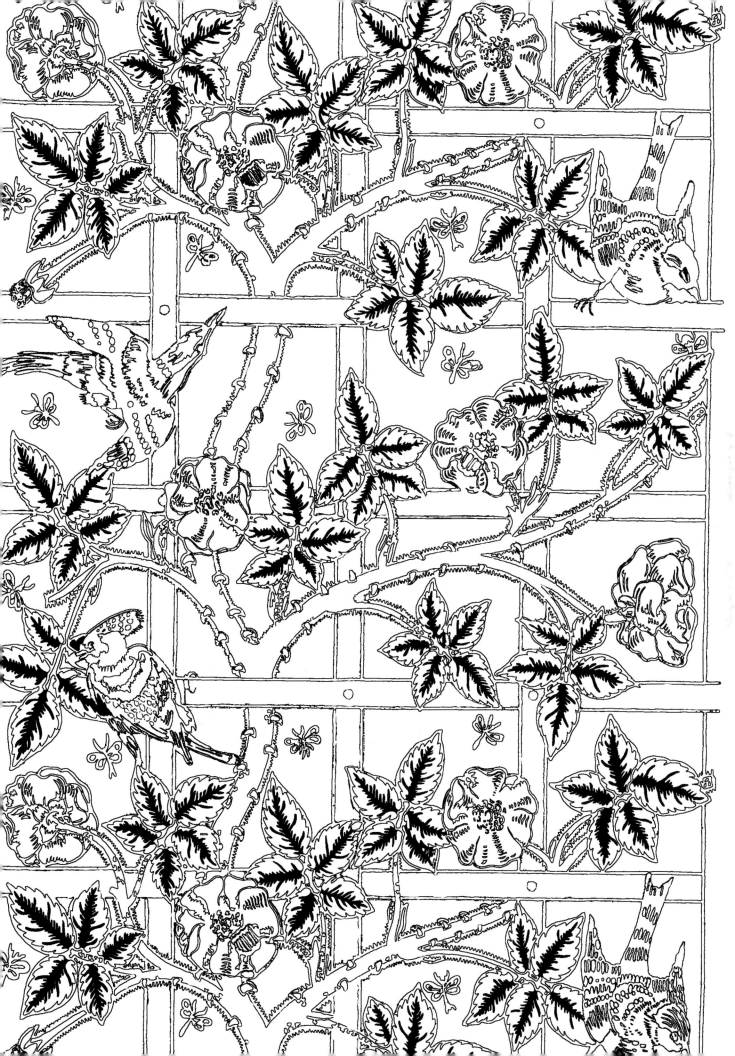

Lily wallpaper

William Morris is recognised today as one of the great masters of flat, repeat-pattern wallpapers. Morris & Co. led the revival of English designed wallpapers in a market that had previously been dominated by French florals on satin grounds. Fashionable interior decoration relied exclusively on wallpapers during the Victorian period. For example, English production had risen from 1.2 million rolls in 1834 to 32 million rolls in 1874.

Morris & Co. wallpapers, while expensive, sold consistently well and *Lily*, designed by Morris in 1874, seems to have been considered by him as a meritorious bedroom wallpaper, the reason being perhaps that, although available in a variety of colours, the effect is simple and meditative with soft shades of green usually forming the ground for pretty clumps of flowering lilies.

Marigold wallpaper

Marigold was first designed as a wallpaper by William Morris in 1875 and is one of the few designs that was used unaltered as a furnishing fabric as well. Printed in single colours such as orange and indigo, Morris relies solely on the flat pattern to hold our visual attention. *Marigold* has a densely floriated ground with strong serpentine sprays of foliage punctuated with large marigold flowers which, simultaneously read as diagonal and vertical elements drawing the eye over the pattern. 🖋

Apple wallpaper

In *The Lesser Arts of Life* (1882) William Morris comments on wallpaper designing as 'quite modern and very humble, but, as things go, useful art.' *Apple* was designed by Morris in 1877 and like *Marigold*, relies on large leaves and apples instead of flowers, to form diagonal rows surrounded by small branches on a white ground. The design is printed in light and dark blue, with the apples given red highlights. Further visual interest is introduced through coloured pin-dotting increasing the density of the apples, while the effect on the leaves is one of light and shade.

The following description, taken from the inside cover of a c.1905 Morris & Co. wallpaper sample book, articulates the firm's desired finish that *Apple* so admirably attains: 'HAND-PRINTED [block-printed] PAPERS are produced very slowly, each block used being dipped into pigment and then firmly pressed on to the paper, giving a great body of colour. This process takes place with each separate colour, which is slowly dried before another is applied. The consequence is that in the finished paper there is a considerable mass of solid colour.'

St James's wallpaper

This wallpaper receives its name from the Royal commission William Morris won to redecorate sections of St James's Palace. The pattern was first issued in 1881 for the palace's Grand Staircase & the Queen's Staircase and is suitably striking in size and formal grandeur. Large acanthus leaves and complex flower-heads dominate the foreground, the effect being pleasantly softened by Morris introducing a meandering underlay of roses, leaves and small flowers on a blue ground.

Printed in distemper colours, with special gold and silver highlights, *St James's* took a staggering sixty-eight blocks to complete. In addition, two widths of paper were required to complete the pattern with its massive vertical repeat of 119.4 cm. This example of *St James's* has the blue ground, but red could also be selected. Both colourings were priced at 32s.6d. a roll, making it Morris & Co.'s most expensive wallpaper, apart from those printed on gold-ground paper. By comparison, Morris & Co.'s standard wallpapers ranged from 3s to 16s.

Bird & anemone wallpaper

Bird & anemone, like the pattern *Marigold*, was available in cotton. However, Morris reduced the size of the pattern repeat to improve its useability as a furnishing and curtain fabric. Morris first issued the design in 1882 and it was available in a number of colours. The bird motif had become an established feature of Morris's fabrics since the late 1870s, and of course, featured in his early wallpaper *Trellis*. Morris's birds in this pattern have a wonderful sense of movement and liveliness captured as they settle on their new-found perches.

Although Morris supplied clients with wallpapers which they could use in any manner they wished, he had quite specific views on its application. In his 1879 lecture 'Making the best of it' and in Wardle's 1883 brochure for the Foreign Fair (Boston) Morris indicates his preference for one pattern per room and a dislike of papered ceilings. *Bird & anemone*, like his other wallpapers, make no pretension to 'architectural features, neither dados, friezes, nor angles' which Morris violently opposed.

Honeysuckle wallpaper

The design was registered in 1883, but it remains unclear if William Morris or his daughter May Morris was responsible for the pattern. Certainly William Morris already had an affinity for using honeysuckle in his designs, producing an elaborate fabric of the same name in 1876. Yet the wallpaper is quite different in feel from the fabric, having a free-flowing pattern of interlacing tendrils on a simple pale-coloured ground. Colour is introduced through the funnel-like tubes of the honeysuckle flower which form bunches in front of an underlay of crisp green leaves. *Honeysuckle* is one of Morris & Co.'s most sensitive and naturalistic wallpaper patterns.

Wild tulip wallpaper

In 1936 May Morris published a book on her father and wrote: 'The character of this design is all Kelmscott to me: the peony and the wild tulip are two of the richest blossomings of the spring garden at the Manor ...'

The fabrics *Wandle* and *Cray* were designed by Morris in mid-1884 and have a strong diagonal meander of stem-flower-stem repeat. *Wild tulip*, registered in November 1884 is the first wallpaper to show this new design characteristic which was to feature prominently in wallpapers thereafter. The pin-dotting seen in *Apple* is taken to new heights in *Wild tulip*, with subtle size, density and colour variations creating a visually dynamic design. Eighteen blocks completed the pattern and a variety of colours, including blue, yellow and red was available.

Willow bough wallpaper

May Morris, in her book (1936) writes: 'We were walking one day by our little stream that runs into the Thames, and my Father pointed out the detail and variety in the leaf forms, and soon afterwards this paper was done, a keenly-observed rendering of our willows that has embowered many a London living-room.'

Willow bough, designed by Morris in 1887, has a structural affinity with the *Honeysuckle* wallpaper of 1883. Refreshingly naturalistic and deceptively simple in construction, both wallpapers de-emphasise the repeat pattern structure. With its gently swaying stems and lightly coloured ground *Willow bough* was extremely popular and the wallpaper enjoyed commercial success for a long period of time.

Pink & rose wallpaper

William Morris designed *Pink & rose* in c.1890 as a simple monochromatic wallpaper available in a wide range of colours. Interior decoration from the late 1880s tended to favour this type of wallpaper over the heavily patterned and multiple coloured papers, which had dominated the 1870s. The pattern has a vertical emphasis created through the upward motion of the flowers and stems of the pinks. Behind are the familiar Tudor roses, however, Morris's abstracted spiky-petalled blossom adds a nice touch of unexpected exoticism.

Carpet

This *Carpet* was probably designed by J. H. Dearle in c.1895; the motifs and structure are an adaptation of William Morris's own carpets. Morris & Co. carpets have two distinct design areas — the border and the centre (known as the field). The border was used to either complement the field or, as we see here, contrast through colour and pattern. The centre pattern is made from radiating circles of formalised flowers, scrolling leaves and tendrils on a blue ground, with the single most important design element being the repetitive use of red to unify the composition. The design of the *Carpet* resembles Persian 'medallion' carpets, so called because of the central medallion with overall symmetrical proportions. Note each quarter of the centre design is the mirror image of its adjoining quarters.

This hand-knotted or 'Hammersmith' carpet was extremely labour-intensive to produce and expensive to purchase. Morris & Co. did offer cheaper machine-woven carpets as well. William Morris first started experimenting with carpet knotting in 1879, in the coach house and stable of Kelmscott House, overlooking the Thames at Hammersmith, hence the name. New larger carpet looms were made when Morris moved to the Merton Abbey workshop in 1881 and young girls seated in rows, on low benches, would make the woven pattern from ready prepared point-paper patterns hanging on their looms. It is not surprising to learn that Morris & Co. considered all of its hand-knotted carpets to be individual works of art.

Swan tile

The *Swan tile* was originally designed by William Morris in 1862 for the border of the tile panel *Sleeping Beauty*. These tiles were hand-painted by Morris, Marshall, Faulkner & Co. onto tin-glazed earthenware Dutch blanks. The *Swan tile* illustrated is entirely Dutch made, possibly by Ravesteijn tileworks, Utrecht, for Morris & Co. Morris probably made contact with tileries in the Netherlands through the London-based Dutch dealer, Murray Marks, who supplied Rossetti and Whistler with old Chinese porcelain which was very fashionable in the 1860s.

    Swan tiles are segmented into grids of sixteen squares of alternating swans and foliage. It is worth observing that the scrolling foliage design, first painted in England in 1862, was altered for the Dutch painted tiles. The Dutch were still hand-painting in traditional methods until the 1880s and these tiles have the soft glossy white and characteristic in-glaze blue that Morris could not achieve with his glass kiln. Tiles such as this were used in the Green Drawing Room fireplace in Kelmscott Manor and Morris also used pure Dutch Delft tiles in his homes. 🖋

Daisy tile

Decorated tiles were not included in the 1861 Morris, Marshall, Faulkner & Co. prospectus until an additional circular was issued in 1862, at which time 'painted earthenware including wall tiles with pictured subjects, figures or patterns' could be ordered. The *Daisy tile* was designed by Morris in 1862 and usually the decoration of the tiles was left to the firm's glass painters and to Charles Faulkner's sisters Kate and Lucy, and Edward Burne-Jones's wife Georgiana. The decorators were restricted to applying low temperature firing enamels to ready glazed tiles as they could only use the firm's glass kiln.

The design for Morris's *Daisy tile* was inspired by the illumination *Dance of the Wodehouses*, a favourite late fifteenth century manuscript Froissart's Chronicles in the British Museum. Froissarts illuminations were reprinted in 1844 and indeed Morris gave a copy of the Chronicles to Louisa Macdonald, Burne-Jones's sister-in-law. The free standing clumps of meadow flowers woven on the medieval hangings illustrated in Froissart, were first translated by Morris onto hangings embroidered by his wife Jane for their master bedroom at Red House in 1860. Morris then developed his *Daisy tile* with its two varieties of foliage and flower petals open or closed. Morris's pattern is a diaper constructed on the diagonal, disregarding the usual horizontal or vertical emphasis imposed by the shape of the tile. So popular was the *Daisy tile* that Morris designed *Daisy* wallpaper in 1864 and although the tile pattern went through a number of variations it remained in stock until 1938.

Adelaide (one of two panels from a screen)

The immensely wealthy Adelaide couple, Robert and Joanna Barr Smith, and their family, were among Morris & Co.'s largest international clients, extensively furnishing seven houses with the firm's products from 1884 to 1929. *Adelaide* is one of several items that Morris & Co. specifically designed and gave an Australian name for the Barr Smith family. The panel design is attributed to May Morris and is embroidered in silks onto a blue silk ground by Joanna's daughter, Erlistoun Mitchell (1868–1913) in c.1890. The panel has two design elements – a heart-shaped daisy-chain and a plant with a large open flower. The curling foliage is in mirror image, with its vertical axis the plant's central flower stem.

William Morris stopped designing embroideries in the 1880s, preferring to leave his daughter, May Morris, to run the embroidery section from 1885 to 1896. During the 1890s William Morris would often visit May in her drawing room, at 8 Hammersmith Terrace, on his way to work to see what her embroideresses were working on. Both May Morris and J. H. Dearle continued to design new embroideries and it is from this period that South Australian families purchased many of their Morris & Co. designs.

Acanthus portière

This elaborate portière, or hanging, was designed by J. H. Dearle and embroidered in South Australia by Mary Isobel Barr Smith (1863–1941) in the 1890s. The design was marked out on the linen and it is likely that the embroidery would have been partially begun, to indicate the types of stitches to be used and their colour placement. Morris & Co. dyed some silks and had others dyed for them; these were then supplied to clients such as Mary. William Morris advocated that his favourite stitches—darning, running, long and short, satin and stem stitches, should be used on all Morris & Co. embroideries. As you can see in the portière the stitches accentuate the lines of the design and never make distracting patterns within themselves, a pet dislike of William Morris's.

The portières of William Morris from the early 1880s are quite different from Dearle's. Morris produced several 'acanthus' hangings that had quartered and halved designs with borders, reflecting the layout he had developed for his hand-knotted carpets. By contrast, Dearle's embroidery designs favoured a loose-flowing pictorial structure. *Acanthus*, along with his contemporaneous designs *Owl and Pigeon*, make effective use of the delicate central flowering tree intertwined by scrolling acanthus leaves.

Tudor rose cushion

The design of the *Tudor rose cushion* is attributed to May Morris and dates from c.1892. The centre of the cushion is dominated by a beautifully embroidered Tudor rose in an array of red tones. Organic tendrils spill out from the edges of the petals, terminating in flowers at each corner. With its central medallion and mirrored quarter patterns, this design is using devices Morris & Co. employed on their carpet patterns.

    The *Morris & Co. Day-book* (1892–96) contains the names of many wealthy-heeled clients. During this period those who were among Morris & Co.'s most prolific customers were Lady Trevelyan, Mrs Ambrose Ralli, Mrs Battye, Mrs Hodson and Mrs Barr Smith (South Australia) who ordered thirty-seven items between them. Mrs Barr Smith ordered one cushion in 1892 for 17/- from Morris & Co. and another two 'started' cushions in 1895 for 16/- and 11/- respectively. Silk embroideries could be purchased in three stages of completion — a kit with fabric, silks and pattern outline; the embroidery partially started to show stitches and colour placement; or as a finished embroidered item. 🖋

Welcome maids of honour fire screen

This design was popular in Adelaide where it was used on a further two fire screens and for a cushion. The design is attributed to May Morris and it was embroidered by an unidentified Adelaide woman in c.1900. The central motif of intertwined roses, is surrounded by a garland of flowers and a band of text which reads: 'Welcome maids of honour you do bring in the spring and wait upon her' taken from the poem *To Violets*, by English poet Robert Herrick (1591–1674). Herrick had something of a revival in late-nineteenth-century England and Australia when Alfred Pollard published *The Works of Robert Herrick* in 1891.

Like May Morris's *Adelaide* panel, the silks are embroidered onto a blue silk ground with a pattern combination of central flower and simple garland. The four corner birds, with their fanned wings and tails relate to embroidered panels that May Morris designed in the mid-1890s. Birds continued to feature regularly in her work during the early twentieth century, most notably in a set of bed-hangings that were designed for a *Women's Guild of Art* project in 1916. 🖋

Table cover

The design of this very fine *Table cover* is attributed to May Morris, with the embroidery in silks being completed by Erlistoun Mitchell (1868–1913) in c.1900. The majority of Morris & Co. table covers have decorative embroidered borders, while this example has an elaborate pattern of floral rings which fan out from the centre. The curling shapes of the vine tendrils in the middle subtly echo the large curved arches that separate the medallion design from the four corner motifs. The circular design was particularly apt for small circular tables and Laurence Hodson of Compton Hall, near Wolverhampton in England, bought the same table cover design in 1895. 🖋

Tulip fabric, 1875; South Australian Government Grant 1990
Crown imperial curtain, 1876; Laurel Phyllis Myers Bequest Fund 1992, Elizabeth Mudge Bequest Fund 1992
Bird curtain, 1878; South Australian Government Grant 1993
Peacock & dragon curtain, 1878; Gift of Mr & Mrs Jock Gosse 1993
Dove & rose curtain, 1879; South Australian Government Grant 1990
Brer rabbit fabric, 1882; Private collection
Windrush fabric, 1883; Gift of Marbury School Inc. 1992
Evenlode curtain, 1883; Gift of William and Lili Manos 1991
Medway curtain, 1885; South Australian Government Grant 1990
Rose & lily curtain, 1893; Gift of Jenny Legoe 2002
Compton curtain, 1896; Gift of Lalla Rymill 1991 and 1993
Trellis wallpaper, 1864; Ellen Christensen Bequest Fund 2002
Lily wallpaper, 1874; Gift of Mr & Mrs Jock Gosse 1990
Marigold wallpaper, 1875; Gift of Mr & Mrs Jock Gosse 1990
Apple wallpaper, 1877; Gift of Haslam & Whiteway Ltd 2002
St James's wallpaper, 1881; Ellen Christensen Bequest Fund 2002
Bird & anemone wallpaper, 1882; Mrs Mary Overton Gift Fund 2000
Honeysuckle wallpaper, 1883; Gift of Mrs J. H. Bagot 1993
Wild tulip wallpaper, 1884; Gift of Marbury School Inc. 1992
Willow bough wallpaper, 1887; Gift of Mr & Mrs Jock Gosse 1990
Pink & rose wallpaper, c.1890; Gift of Mr & Mrs Jock Gosse 1990
Carpet, c.1895; Gift of Mr & Mrs Jock Gosse and the Jean Smith Bequest Fund 1999
Swan tile, 1862; The Walker Lowe Collection, Gift 1993
Daisy tile, c.1862; Mrs Mary Overton Gift Fund 2002
Adelaide panel, c.1890; Private collection
Acanthus portière, 1890s; Gift of Mr & Mrs Jock Gosse 1996
Tudor rose cushion, c.1892; Private collection
Fire screen, c.1900 ; South Australian Government Grant 1997
Table cover, c.1900; Private collection

Text written by Robert Reason
Edited by Penelope Curtin
Designed by Antonietta Itropico
Film and outlines by van Gastel Graphics Pty Ltd, Adelaide, South Australia, Australia
Printed by van Gastel Printing Pty Ltd, Adelaide, South Australia, Australia

National Cataloguing-in-Publication data

Robert Reason
Morris & Co. : designs & patterns from the Art Gallery of South Australia.

ISBN 0 7308 3037 3.

1. Morris, William, 1834-1896. 2. Morris & Co. (London,
England). 3. Art Gallery of South Australia. 4. Decorative arts –
Great Britain – 19th century. 5. Arts and crafts movement –
South Australia. I. Art Gallery of South Australia. II. Title.

745.44941

Art Gallery of South Australia

North Terrace, Adelaide, South Australia 5000
ph: 61 8 8207 7000 facs: 61 8 8207 7070
www.artgallery.sa.gov.au